DATE DUE

| | | | |
|---|---|---|---|
| | | | |
| | | | |
| | | | |
| | | | |
| | | | |
| | | | |
| | | | |
| | | | |
| | | | |
| | | | |
| | | | |

DEMCO

# Robert Nathaniel's Tree

Library of Congress Catalog No. 92-076071
ISBN 0-9630017-3-6

Design: Julie Toffaletti, Montgomery, Alabama
Printing: Father & Son Associates, Inc., Tallahassee, Florida

Dedicated to my husband, Thomas Robert Schlitt, and to my wonderful children: Thomas Alexander, Virginia Elise, Robert Nathaniel, and Marjorie Adair. My special thanks to everyone who aided in this project, particularly Lucy Blount, Cam Armstrong, and Julie Toffaletti. And I thank God for many answered prayers.

RaRa Sartwell Schlitt


To Emma and Jerry, who I love more than you'll ever know, and to all those whose prayers helped bring this effort to completion.

Camilla Brunschwyler Armstrong

For He shall give His angels charge over thee,
to keep thee in all thy ways.

PSALM 91:11

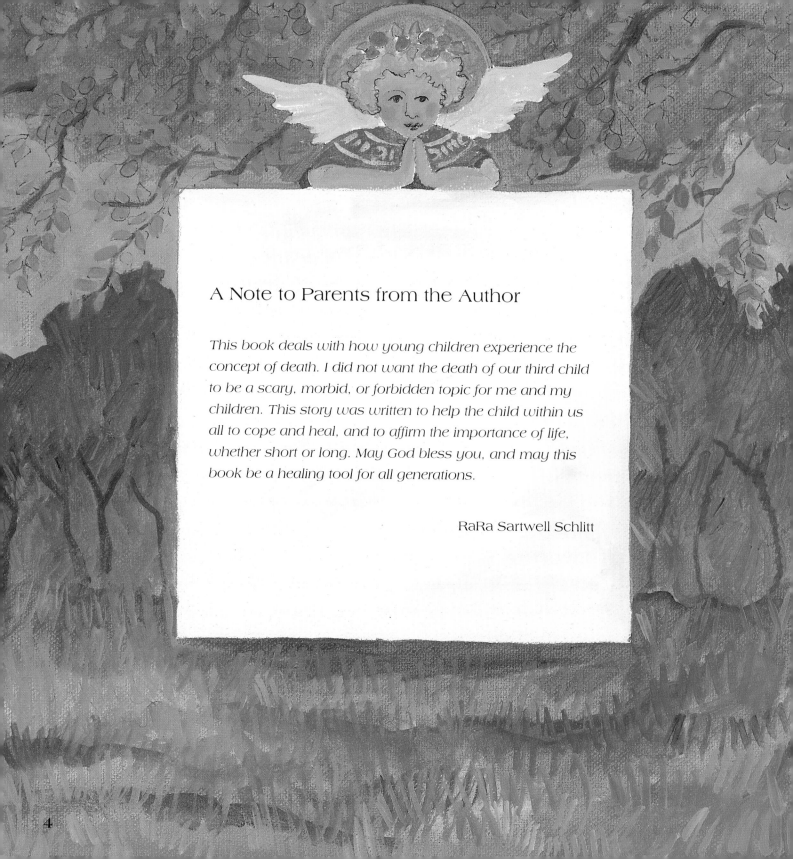

## A Note to Parents from the Author

*This book deals with how young children experience the concept of death. I did not want the death of our third child to be a scary, morbid, or forbidden topic for me and my children. This story was written to help the child within us all to cope and heal, and to affirm the importance of life, whether short or long. May God bless you, and may this book be a healing tool for all generations.*

RaRa Sartwell Schlitt

# Robert Nathaniel's Tree

By
Ra Ra Sartwell Schlitt

Illustrated by
Camilla Brunschwyler Armstrong

5

I like popsicles, catching raindrops in my mouth, and feeling the baby move in Mommy's tummy.

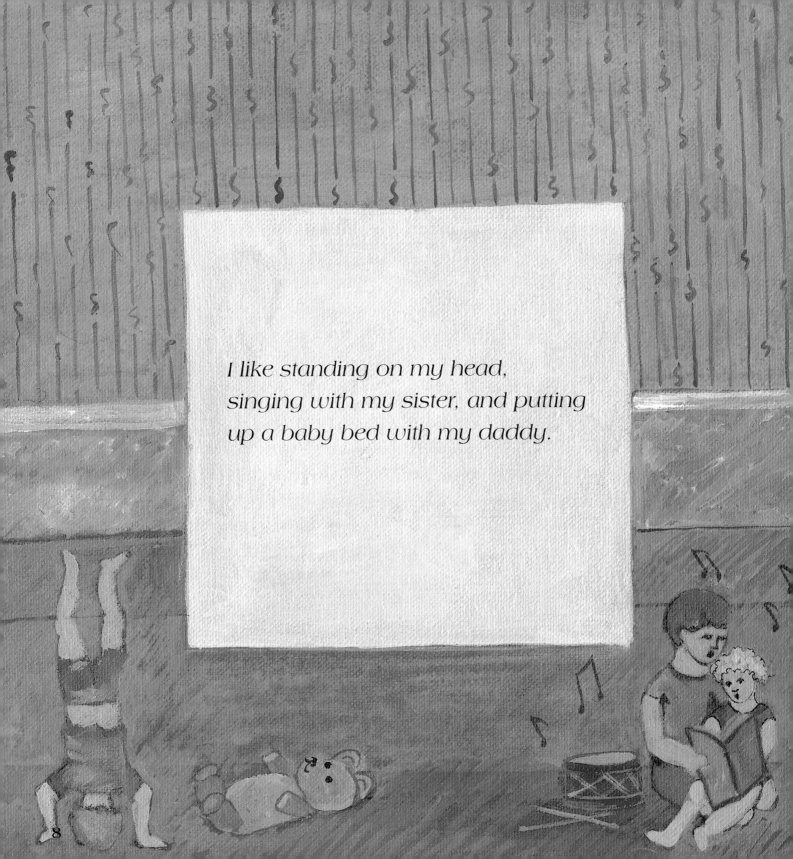

I like standing on my head,
singing with my sister, and putting
up a baby bed with my daddy.

8

9

*I like bedtime stories, catching fireflies in empty mayonnaise jars, and telling Mommy and Daddy to name the new baby, "Frog."*

10

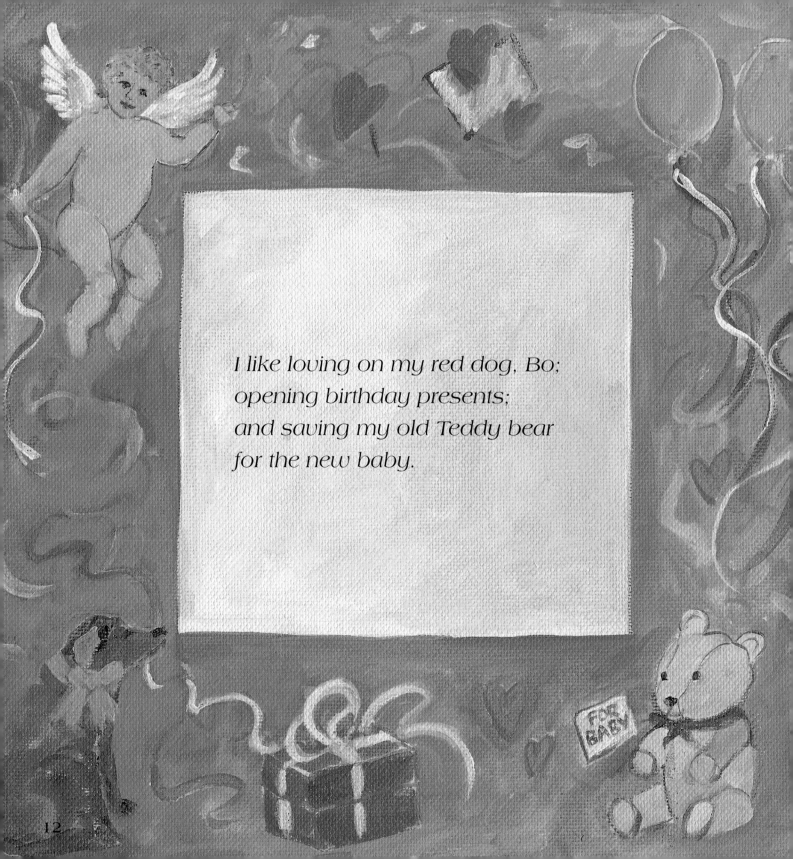

I like loving on my red dog, Bo;
opening birthday presents;
and saving my old Teddy bear
for the new baby.

I like swinging real high,
going to the circus, and eating
ice cream with Mommy.

I like helping Mommy pack her bags for the hospital, drawing a picture for the new baby, and getting ready to visit them both.

But our baby died.

I don't like that.

I don't like seeing Mommy and Daddy sad, and how everyone whispers when I'm around.

I don't like watching Mommy and Daddy take down the nursery, and seeing them put away the stuffed animals.

I don't like not getting to tickle
his toes or play peek-a-boo.

I don't like it that we didn't get to
play ball together or wait up for
Santa Claus.

I don't like it that our baby died
and isn't at home with me.

23

Daddy said his name was
Robert Nathaniel.

I like that.

24

I like it that Mommy and Daddy planted a tree for Robert Nathaniel, and let me take care of it.

I like watering Robert Nathaniel's tree, showing it flowers, and lying on my back beside it to see heaven.

I like getting taller like Robert Nathaniel's tree and showing it my green shirt and brown shoes.

The Secret Garden

27

I like taking care of
Robert Nathaniel's tree.

But I miss my little brother.

Sometimes trees live.
Sometimes trees die.

Sometimes babies live.
Sometimes babies die.

31

I like eating ice cream and cake and remembering Robert Nathaniel.

I like it that Robert Nathaniel has a tree and that songbirds have built a nest in it.

I love being Robert Nathaniel's big brother.

Even if he didn't come home.

And we know that all things
work together for good to them
that love God, to them who
are called according to
His purpose.

ROMANS 8:28